THIS BOOK BELONGS TO

____

AIME Publishing LLC
Alpharetta, GA

Written by I & A Seddawy
Illustrated by Natalia Kapatsoulia
Edited by Robin Katz
Book design by Arlene Soto, Intricate Designs

Names: Seddawy, I., author. | Seddawy, A., author. | Kapatsoulia, Natalia, illustrator.
Title: The legend of Osiris : a story of love and family / written by I & A Seddawy ; illustrated by Natalie Kapatsoulia.
Description: Alpharetta, GA : AIME Publishing LLC, [2025] | Series: Noah and Mia tales of the Nile. | Audience: ages 5 to 8. | Summary: When Noah and Mia open a mysterious book in their grandmother's library, a flash of golden light whisks them to Ancient Egypt. Guided by the wise Thoth, they join the Legend of Osiris, a brave king betrayed by his brother Seth. Alongside Queen Isis, they learn that the power of love, courage, and family can overcome even the greatest evil.--Publisher.
Identifiers: LCCN: 2025917960 | ISBN: 9798900308401 (paperback) | 9798900308418 (hardcover) | 9798900308388 (eBook)
Subjects: LCSH: Osiris (Egyptian deity)--Juvenile fiction. | Isis (Egyptian deity)--Juvenile fiction. | Thoth (Egyptian deity)--Juvenile fiction. | Love--Mythology--Juvenile fiction. | Egypt--Civilization--To 332 B.C.--Juvenile fiction. | Families--Juvenile fiction. | Courage--Juvenile fiction. | Good and evil--Juvenile fiction. | CYAC: Osiris (Egyptian deity)--Fiction. | Isis (Egyptian deity)--Fiction. | Thoth (Egyptian deity)--Fiction. | Love--Mythology--Fiction. | Egypt--Fiction. | Families--Fiction. | Courage--Fiction. | Good and evil--Fiction. | LCGFT: Historical fiction. | BISAC: JUVENILE FICTION / Historical / Ancient Civilizations. | JUVENILE FICTION / Action & Adventure / General. | JUVENILE FICTION / Family / General.
Classification: LCC: PZ7.1.S33697 L44 2025 | DDC: [E]--dc23

The LEGEND of OSIRIS

A STORY OF LOVE AND FAMILY

WRITTEN BY
I & A SEDDAWY

ILLUSTRATED BY
NATALIA KAPATSOULIA

AN ADVENTURE AWAITS

Noah and Mia always knew there was something special about their grandma, Téta. Egypt lived in her stories, in the treasures tucked around her home, and in the way her eyes sparkled whenever she spoke about its long, rich history.

The two siblings always looked forward to visiting Téta. In her house, their favorite place of all was the library. Every shelf seemed to be packed with secrets, myths, heroes, and magic waiting for someone to discover.

Whenever Noah and Mia stepped inside, it felt like entering a world where anything could happen. One evening, while visiting Téta, they tiptoed between the tall bookshelves of her library. The lamplight flickered softly as their fingers brushed over worn, cracked covers. Then something unusual caught their eye.

A dusty, antique-looking book sat nearly hidden in a dark corner.

Noah and Mia stared at the old leather cover. Golden symbols glowed along the spine, as if the book itself was breathing with light. It looked like it was holding a secret, one that had been hidden for a long time, waiting to be revealed.

Noah traced the glowing shapes with his finger, while Mia tried to pull the cover open. "Here, help me!" she whispered.

Together, they opened the book as a strange warmth rushed through the air. A golden scarab drawn on the page began to shine, and suddenly, a swirl of golden sand began to rise from the floor, wrapping them in a dazzling spiral of light.

"*Whoa!* What is happening?" Mia gasped, gripping Noah's arm.

Before Noah could answer, a gust of wind swept past their faces. The book trembled in their hands. Sand spilled from the pages like it was pouring from a hidden hourglass.

"I think we're going on an adventure!" Noah shouted.

When the sand finally settled, they were no longer in the library.

Noah and Mia realized they had just landed in Ancient Egypt.

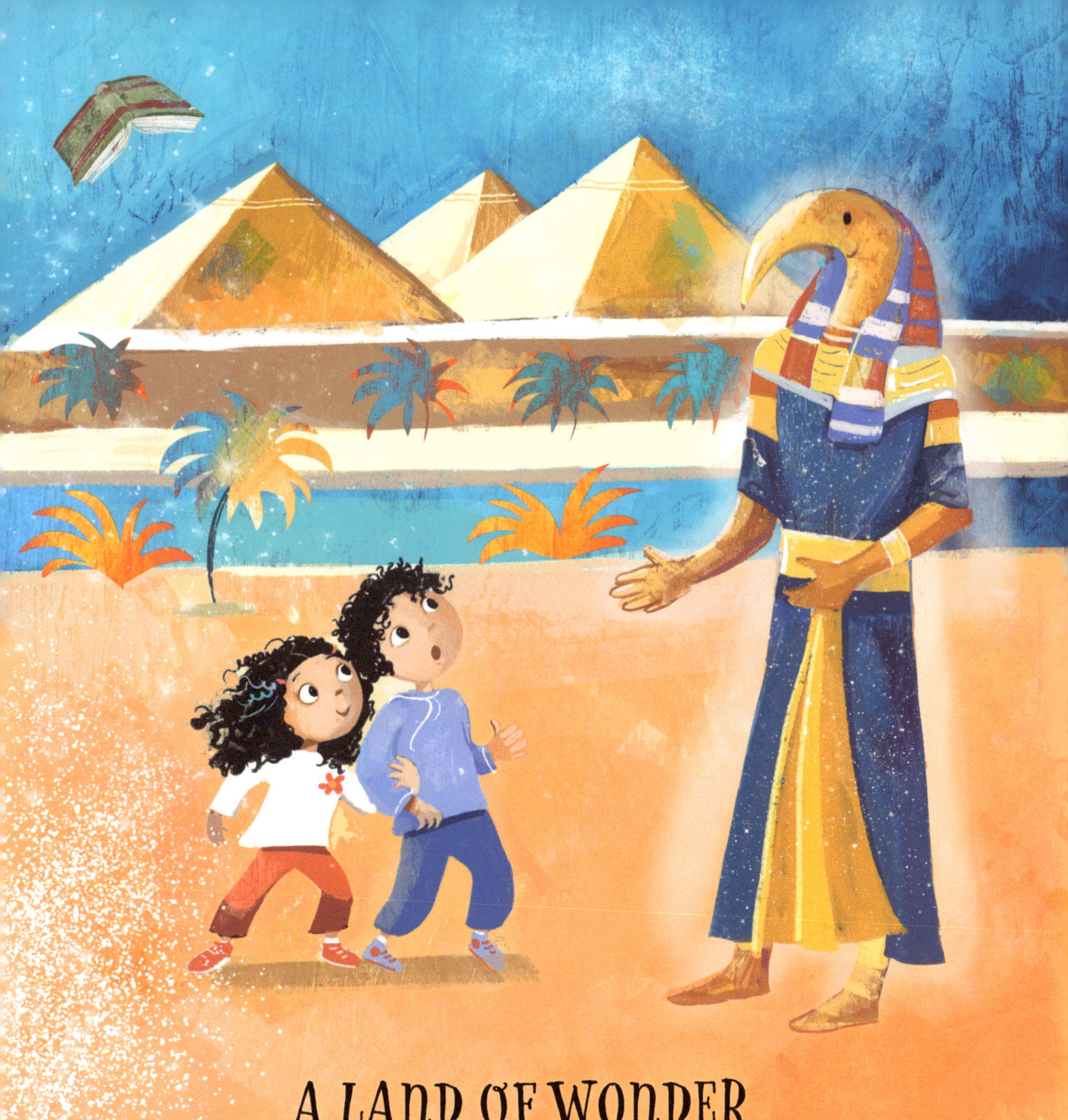

A LAND OF WONDER

In hushed awe, Noah and Mia stared at the golden pyramids rising against the horizon and the shimmering Nile River below. Mia bent down to touch the cool water flowing past her fingers.

"It's real," she whispered.

"Should we follow the river?" Noah asked.

Before Mia could answer, a tall figure appeared before them. They looked up to find a man with the head of an ibis bird welcoming them with open arms.

His robe sparkled with deep blue and silver colors like stars in the night sky.

"I am Thoth, the wise and knowing Storyteller of the Gods," he proclaimed in a deep voice that echoed with power and mystery.

Thoth continued, "Welcome to Memphis, the capital of the Old Kingdom of Egypt. You have come to witness the special story of Isis and Osiris, and I shall guide you through it, every step of the way. Follow me."

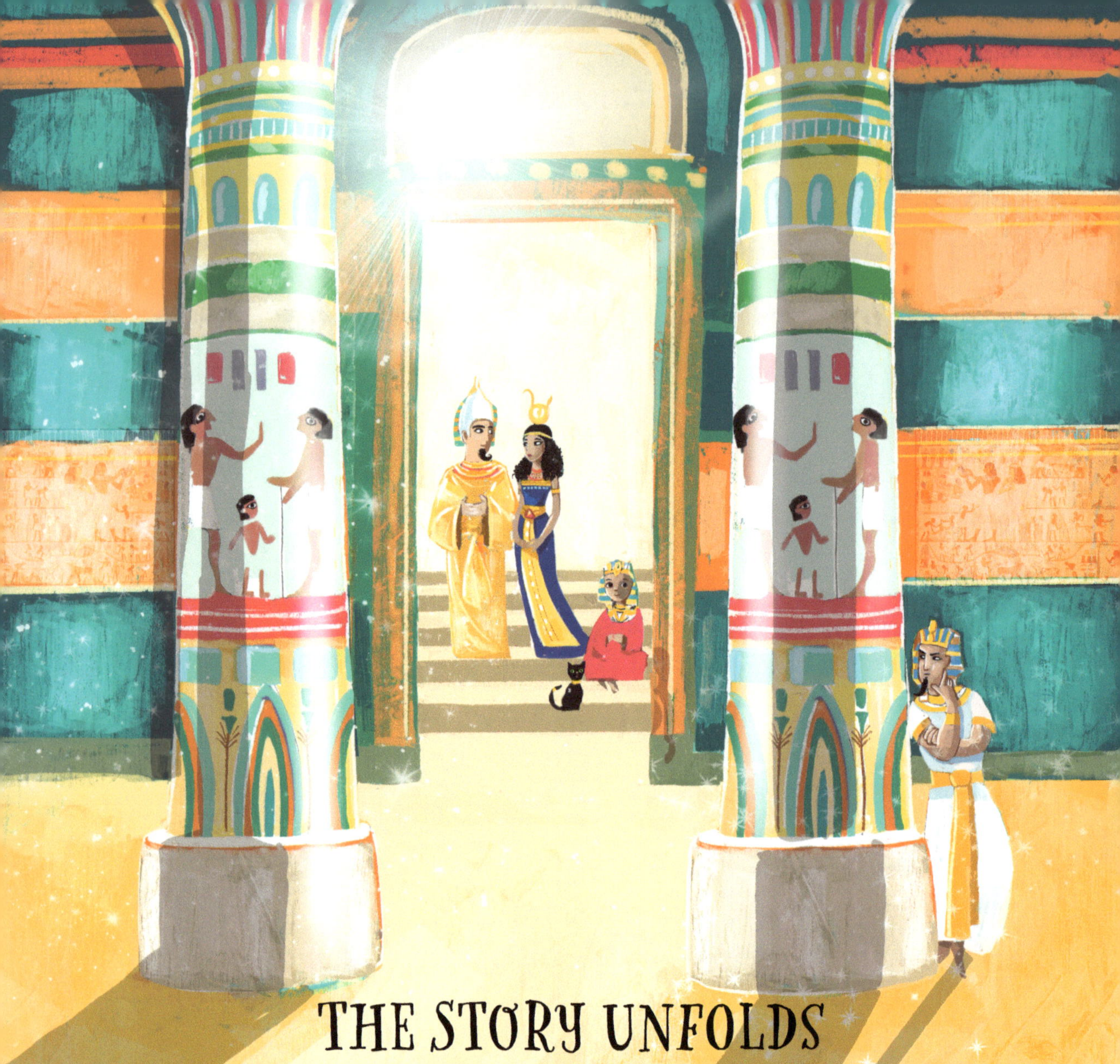

THE STORY UNFOLDS

Thoth led Noah and Mia through tall golden gates into a magnificent royal palace. Beautiful paintings of gods and pharaohs graced the walls, bursting with rich, vibrant colors.

Decorated columns rose high from floor to ceiling, their tops shaped like blooming lotus flowers. At the heart of the grand hall stood Osiris, a noble and wise king. His long, golden robe shimmered brightly like the sun.

Beside him stood his wife, Queen Isis, her eyes warm with love and kindness. She wore a flowing dark blue dress, the color of the sacred Nile River. A golden crown rested upon her head, sparkling softly in the sunlight. Nearby stood their young son, Horus, always watching everything with curious eyes.

King Osiris and Queen Isis ruled Egypt with fairness and respect, and the people loved them. But hidden in the shadows, someone was watching with jealousy.

Osiris' younger brother, Seth, stood quietly, his hands clenched tight, eyes burning with envy.

Seth longed to be king and dreamed of taking the throne for himself. An evil smile spread across his face as he began to set a secret plan in motion.

THE TRICK OF SETH

That evening at the royal court, noblemen and high priests gathered to celebrate *Opet*, the festival of gods. During the ceremony, Seth presented a stunning wooden chest decorated with precious jewels that sparkled like stars.

"Whoever fits inside this chest perfectly may keep it!" Seth announced, his voice smooth like a serpent's whisper.

Intrigued, the members of the court gathered around. One by one, they stepped inside, but none of them could perfectly fit. At last, Osiris stepped forward, smiling as he admired his brother's fine craftsmanship.

"Let me try," the king said as he carefully climbed inside the golden chest, unaware of Seth's evil trick.

The moment Osiris lay down, Seth slammed the lid shut, as a flash of dark magic surged around the chest, locking it with a powerful force.

"You shall never rule again, brother," Seth proclaimed, his voice filled with hate. With a wave of his hand, his guards lifted the chest and carried it away.

A sense of fear and betrayal quickly spread through the court. Before anyone could stop them, Seth's followers lowered the chest into the mighty Nile River, where the deep waters carried it away.

"Oh no!" Mia gasped. "What will happen to Osiris?"

Then her eyes lit up. "I have an idea! Let's follow Isis and help her find the chest."

Noah nodded. "We should go right now! We cannot waste any time!"

Thoth looked at them with calm approval. "The two of you are showing great courage." He said gently. "Come with me, and you will witness Isis' journey as she travels far and wide to reunite with her husband."

ISIS NEVER GIVES UP

With Osiris taken away, Isis' eyes filled with tears, but she refused to give up. She had to find him. Day and night, Isis looked for the king, crossing hot deserts where the sand burned beneath her feet.

She climbed tall mountains where the winds whistled through the rocks. At night, Isis would whisper to the moon and stars, asking for help, as they twinkled back, guiding her way.

Through wind and rain, Isis never stopped searching.

At last, after a long journey, she found Osiris' chest hidden in the sand far away in a distant land.

Her heart was filled with hope as she rushed to open the chest. But before she could reach it, Seth used his evil magic again to vanish the chest and keep them apart.

Mia squeezed Noah's hand. "Thoth," she whispered, "did Isis lose hope and give up on her quest to find Osiris?"

Thoth smiled gently. "No," he said. "She did not give up. Love never gives up."

Knowing she could not do this alone, Isis called upon Anubis, the wise and powerful guardian of the gods. Anubis appeared with the body of a man and the head of a black jackal. Calm and gentle, he helped protect the people of Egypt and maintain peace across the Kingdom.

With Anubis beside her, Isis used his sacred powers to cast her magic. Ancient symbols floated through the air as she whispered spells of healing and protection, her heart filled with hope.

At last, Osiris opened his eyes, surrounded by a warm golden light. Though he would no longer rule as king on Earth, he was given a new purpose in another world where he would spread peace, wisdom, and goodwill.

A NEW KING RISES

Meanwhile, Isis raised their son, Horus, teaching him courage, loyalty, and kindness. As he grew older, Horus learned how to rule the people he loved and the land he vowed to protect.

Once Horus was ready to become king, he faced Seth to restore peace to Egypt and take his father's throne back.

Throughout this epic journey, the *Eye of Horus* glowed with Osiris' divine strength and the power of trust from the people of Egypt. Horus and Seth battled fiercely, light against darkness, good fighting evil.

At last, with great bravery and the support of Anubis, Isis, and the Kingdom that stood beside him, Horus triumphed. Seth was sent into a faraway land from where he could never return, and with that, peace was finally restored to the Land of the Pharaohs.

Horus was crowned the new and rightful king of Egypt, and he watched over his people with fairness and justice. The *Eye of Horus* became, and remains, a symbol of strength, protection, and family bonds, guiding the Kingdom of Egypt for generations to come.

BACK HOME

As the story came to an end, Noah and Mia noticed the golden light of the scarab swirling around them once again. Just as they felt themselves being gently pulled away, a familiar voice echoed through the shimmering mist of sand.

"You have witnessed a great tale of love and courage," Thoth said. His eyes gleamed with warmth as he waved farewell. "And now, your journey must go on."

Mia clutched the book to her chest, her heart still racing. "Isis never gave up on Osiris," she whispered.

"And love is what makes a family strong," Noah added, his voice filled with wonder and excitement. "No matter where you go, that love stays with you, just like it did for Isis and Osiris."

Thoth smiled gently. "Remember this, young travelers: love, courage, and family will always light your way. Even in the hardest times, these values will forever be there to guide you through life."

   The golden scarab rose from the book and began to shine brightly. Thoth's face slowly faded, along with the pyramids and the Nile River behind him. A soft breeze swept around Noah and Mia, and in the blink of an eye, they found themselves back in Téta's library. The tall bookshelves stood quietly around them, just as before, but magic was still in the air.

   Noah and Mia felt a gentle warmth in their hearts as they thought about the story they had just witnessed, and the lessons learned along the way. They were happy to be home, but sad that their journey with Thoth had reached its final chapter.

   Noah and Mia dreamed of their next adventure. To be sure they would find their way back to Thoth and Ancient Egypt, Noah scribbled a note: *The Tale of the Nile begins here. Look for the golden scarab.* He slipped it inside the front cover and placed the book back on the shelf as the scarab's glow faded away.

Noah and Mia looked at each other and wondered where the book's magic would take them next.

They could hardly wait to find out!

GODS & GODDESSES OF EGYPT

~OSIRIS~

He is the god of new beginnings. Osiris was a kind and wise king who taught people how to farm and live in peace. He was loved by everyone, but his jealous brother, Seth, tricked him and took his place.

Osiris is shown wearing a tall white crown and holding a special crook and flail, known as symbols of his care and strength.

~ISIS~

She is the goddess of magic, healing, and love. Isis was a powerful and caring queen known for her bravery and wisdom. She loved her husband Osiris deeply and used her magic to bring him back when he was tricked by Seth.

Isis is also the protector of children and mothers. She is often shown with a throne-shaped crown on her head and magical wings that shine like the stars. Her symbol is the ankh, which stands for life.

⟿HORUS⟿

He is the god of the sky and protector of Egypt. Horus was the brave and powerful son of Isis and Osiris. He had the head of a falcon and eyes that sparkled like the sun and moon.

Horus fought to bring peace and justice after his father, Osiris, was tricked by Seth. He is often shown wearing a crown while flying high in the sky, watching over the land. His symbol is the Eye of Horus, which stands for protection and strength.

⟿THOTH⟿

He is the god of wisdom, writing, and the moon. Thoth was clever and calm, always helping gods and people solve problems. He invented writing and kept important stories, knowledge, and secrets safe.

Thoth is often shown with the head of an ibis bird, holding a scroll or a writing tool. He was known as a gentle guide who helped protect balance and order in the world. His symbol is the moon, which glows softly in the night sky.

~SETH~

He is the god of chaos, deserts, and storms. Seth was strong and powerful, but he was jealous of his brother, King Osiris. He caused trouble among the gods by trying to take over Egypt.

Even though he made mistakes, Seth was sometimes called on to protect the sun during its journey through the night. He is shown with a mysterious animal head, unlike any other creature, and his symbol is the storm.

~ANUBIS~

He is the wise and powerful guardian of the gods. Anubis helps protect the people of Egypt and maintain peace across the Kingdom. Calm and gentle, he watches over others with care and fairness.

Anubis is shown with the body of a man and the head of a black jackal. His symbol is a scale, which reminds people to choose kindness, balance, and respect in their hearts.

~AMUN-RA~

He is the great god of the sun and air. Amun-Ra was a mix of two powerful gods: Amun, who was quiet like the wind, and Ra, who brought light to the world.

Together, Amun and Ra became King of Gods. Amun-Ra helped create everything and watched over the people of Egypt. He is often shown with a tall crown and a glowing sun. His symbol is the sun shining in the sky.

~HATHOR~

She is the goddess of love, music, and joy. Hathor was kind and full of happiness. She helped people feel love and comfort, and she brought music and dancing to the world.

Hathor is often shown with a sun between cow horns on her head, and her smile could brighten anyone's day. Her symbol is the sistrum, a musical rattle that brings joy.

ᴖNUITᴖ

She is the goddess of the sky and stars. Nuit stretched across the sky like a big, shining blanket covered in stars. She gently watched over the earth and kept everyone safe at night.

Each evening, Nuit brought out the moon and helped the sun rest until morning. She was loving and gentle. Her symbol is the night sky filled with stars.

ᴖMA'ATᴖ

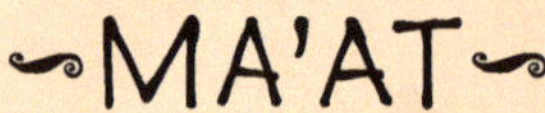

She is the goddess of truth, balance, and fairness. Ma'at helped keep the world peaceful and made sure everyone tried to do what was right.

Ma'at wore a feather on her head, a symbol of truth and order.

~BASTET~

She is the goddess of protection, home, and joy. Bastet was gentle and caring, always bringing comfort and happiness to families. She loved music, dancing, and celebration.

Bastet is often shown with the head of a cat, and she protected people from harm. Her symbol is the cat, graceful and strong.

~BES~

He is the protector of homes, laughter, and sleep. Bes was small and funny-looking, but very strong! He loved to make people laugh and helped scare away bad dreams. Families believed Bes kept children safe while they slept.

Bes danced, played music, and made every home feel warm and happy. His symbol is a drum or tambourine, full of fun and joy.

CAN YOU WRITE YOUR NAME LIKE AN ANCIENT EGYPTIAN PHARAOH?

The ancient Egyptians did not use letters like we do today. They used pictures called **hieroglyphs**!

Look at the chart on the right. Each picture stands for a sound or letter.

NOW TRY THIS:

1. **Find the letters of your name** in the chart.

2. **Draw the hieroglyphs** that match your name inside the big royal oval (called a cartouche).

3. **Add your own decorations!** Make it colorful, sparkly, or even magical!

DID YOU KNOW? Ancient Egyptians believed writing your name in a cartouche gave it **protection and power!**

So go ahead! Write your name like a Pharaoh!

Aa Bb Cc Dd Ee Ff Gg Hh Ii Jj
Kk Ll Mm Nn Oo Pp Qq Rr Ss Tt
Uu Vv Ww Xx Yy Zz TH SH CH KH

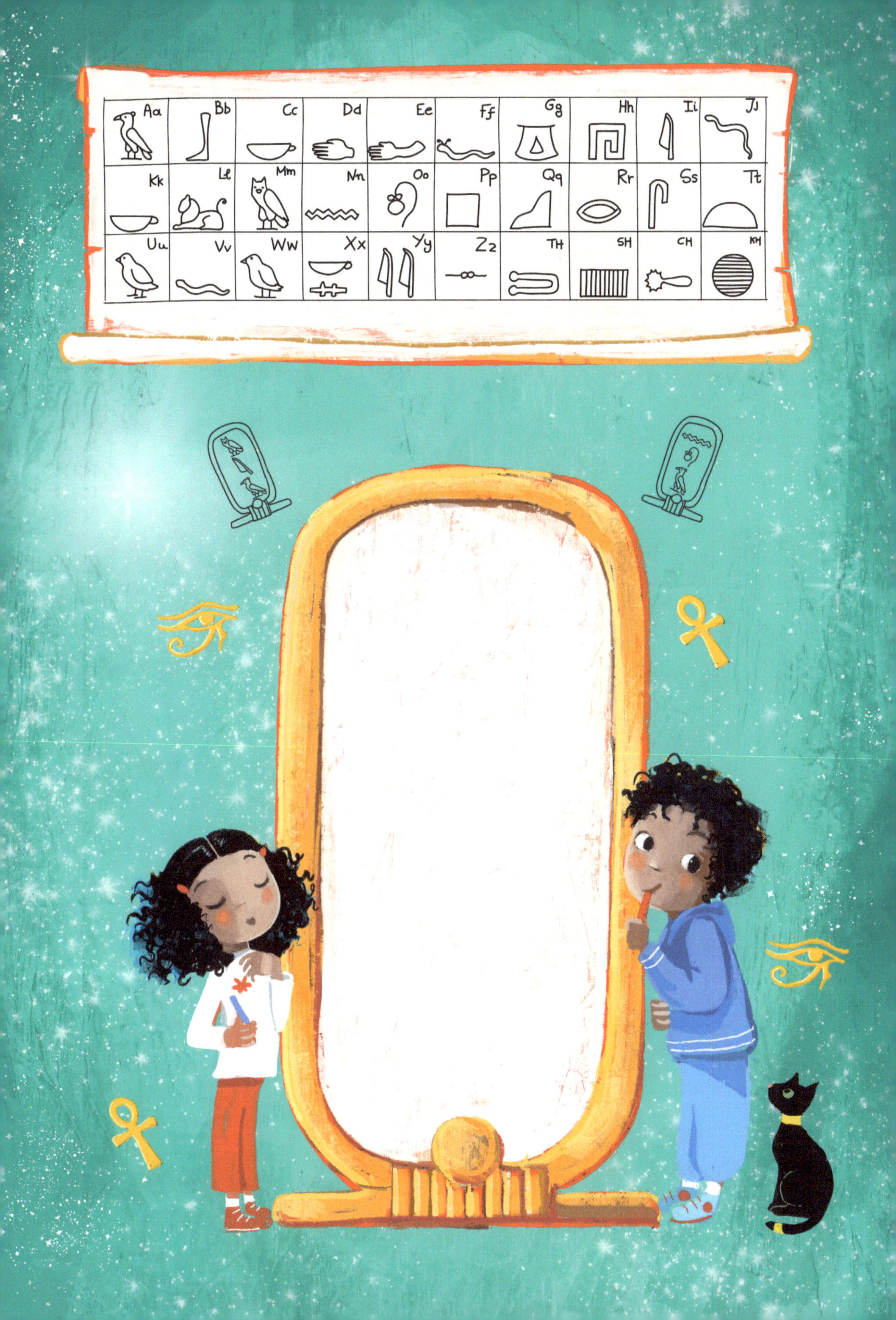

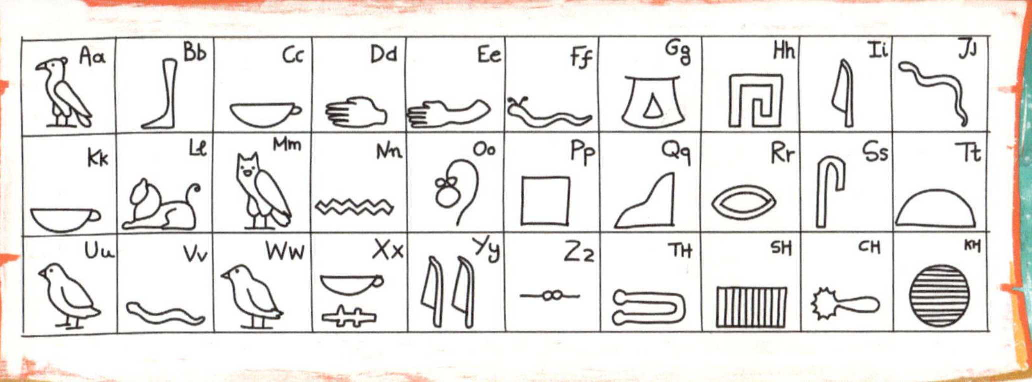

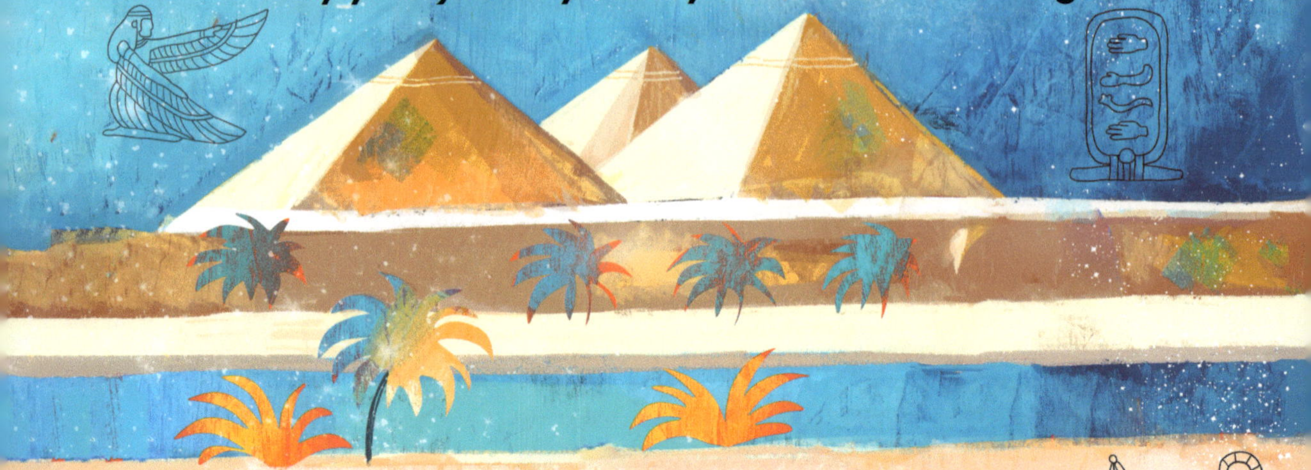

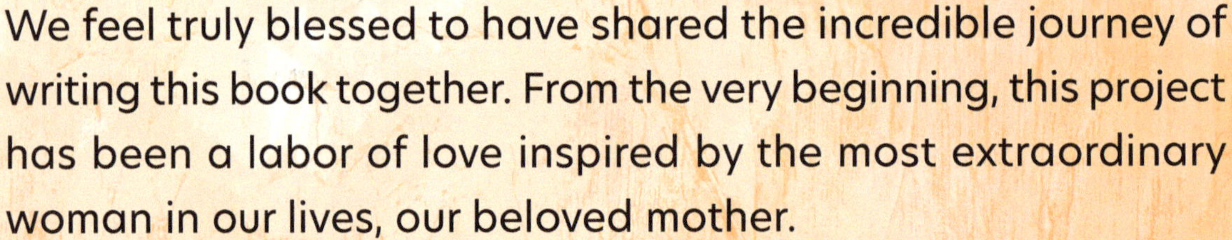

A NOTE FROM THE AUTHORS

We feel truly blessed to have shared the incredible journey of writing this book together. From the very beginning, this project has been a labor of love inspired by the most extraordinary woman in our lives, our beloved mother.

Over the years, we came to think of our mother as the greatest storyteller of all time. As children, we would gather around her, completely captivated by the mesmerizing tales of ancient Egypt she brought to life.

Our mother's voice carried the magic of the pharaohs, the secrets of the pyramids, and the whispers of a time long past. Today, she shares those stories with our children, filling them with the same sense of marvel and curiosity that once captivated us.

A devoted Egyptologist, our mother has dedicated her life to sharing the wonders of Egypt with others. She has been a pioneer, opening doors to a world of history and magic for so many.

Some of our most treasured memories are visiting the pyramids with our mother and hearing her bring history to life at the Egyptian Museum. Those moments sparked a deep love for our heritage that still lives within us. Now that we are far from Egypt, we see that same light in our children when they listen to her stories. Their wonder and excitement inspired us to write this book and share those untold tales with the world.

These are not the common stories found in most mythology books. They were passed down by someone who has truly lived and breathed Egypt's history. Through her lens as an Egyptologist, our mother has infused each tale with rich details, personal insight, and imagination, inviting readers to immerse themselves in these mystical yet authentic legends.

If the magic of ancient Egypt has ever whispered to your imagination, and you have dreamed of wandering through its grand temples or walking in the footsteps of the pharaohs, we invite you to enjoy this journey with us.

-I & A

Follow Us @noahandmiatales
naohandmiatales@gmail.com
www.noahandmiatales.com